SELF

INTRODUCTION

How to Answer "Tell Me about Yourself"

By

LIZZY JONES

CONTENT

PREFACE

A good Self-introduction is what everyone must do at a particular time in his or her life in other to be part of a particular system with the overall purpose of achieving success.

This book is put together to help people pull through the initial fear and anxiety that usually engulfs inexperienced public speakers and job seekers who are most affected by the trauma associated with poor self-introduction.

With a precise definition, the author explains self-introduction tricks with practical examples on how to introduce self in a job interview, public presentation, and new connection and in writing a letter of self-introduction.

You'll learn how to write a winning resume and other things you need to know about a professional introduction.

Then the dreaded question of "Tell me more about yourself" – how to prepare your response and answering the question; with an in-depth analysis of what to and what not to say in responding to this question.

You'll also learn how you can introduce yourself in a formal group discussion.

Ending with self-motivational quotes of all time the author could be said to have simply provided everything you need to succeed in public speaking and presentation.

SELF-INTRODUCTION

A self-introduction ought to include a name, occupation, and things like interests, values, etc that will assist in making the desired impression on your target. Possibly the person you're talking to or the audience. As a general rule, you must be clear and outspokenly laud during a self-introduction; and in a short statement you're expected to say correctly, What you want people to know about you,

What precisely is self-introduction?

If you ask me I will say it's an attempt to explain who you are, your occupation, and what you want others to know about you. It usually occurs anytime there's a meeting between you and someone else or you and a group of persons.☐

Notably, we can talk about a job interview, social gathering, public forums, and new connections, during a presentation, meeting clients on a business date as some of the places that compulsorily requires a self-introduction, though some informal meetings will still require a self-introduction. □

Self-Introduction Tricks

A well-composed expression will not only help you make new friends it will enable you to learn more about who you are. When you don't have anybody to tell your story, you must strive to tell the story yourself and the best story about yourself begins with a self-introduction. So whenever the need arises, remember to make it appealing and unforgettable. □

Doing it right must be emphasized because there's usually no time for a second chance you can hear people talk about the first impression, which they say matters a lot.

> **You can write down and study an introduction about yourself before the presentation.**

Regardless of whether you want to deliver it or read it out in a speech, it may be worthwhile to draft it out so that you can practice, memorize and be familiar with what you want to say to avoid omitting important facts. □

These steps may be useful in writing or delivering a good self-introduction:-.

1. Precise professional Background
2. your experiences and achievements
3. your interest as a lead-in to the main discussion

Precise professional Background

You should begin self-introduction with your name, depending on the occasion, job title or qualification could follow. If it's a job interview, for instance, you should include educational   Qualifications, certifications, or current job status. I will give two examples:

Unemployed persons job interview –

"My name is Pamela Smith, and I'm a fresh mass communication graduate from the University of Chicago."□

Employed person's job interview-

"My name is Pamela Smith, and I'm a human interest

editor for Norrander consults."□

. Your Experiences and Achievements

This pattern aims to highlight very important details about self to the person you're speaking to or your audience. In a job interview, for instance, you talk about your professional skills and accomplishments.

If you're talking to an audience, you can say something that reinforces your authority in the subject matter under discussion. Thus, you're introducing yourself with an emphasis on what you can offer.

Example of a job interview

-"My name is Pamela Smith, and I'm seeking an experienced- level Editorial job that will enable me to utilize my attention to detail, organization and time management skills."

Your interest as a lead-in to the main discussion

Your concern here is to let your audience know of the unique interest that you have on the subject that you're talking about. By this, you're already telling them what you want them to know. In doing the introduction it should also reflect a call for action.

In an interview situation, for instance, say exactly what they want to hear by indicating that you're the most qualified person for the job. And be ready to take the next question that could come as an offshoot of your claim.

> **Below are written Self-introduction templates**

These sample templates are available here to help self-presenters practice before the presentation, or for those sending a written self-introduction. Four samples of everyday situations that people encounter are as follows: Self-introduction for a **job** interview, for a **presentation**, for Public **forums** and new **connection**, and a written sample

Self-introduction for a job interview

"My name is Pamela Smith. I'm a fresh mass communication graduate from the University of Chicago. I've been functioning as an editor for Norrander consults this year, and I'm eager to get my first TV news

editing position in this reputable firm. I have many, on the job knowledge of live TV news editing styles, which, I acquired during my industrial attachment program at CNN, which, I look forward to implementing in your company. I anchored a lot of broadcasts myself and believe I would be a great fit for your TV station. It would be a thing of joy for me to practice my lifetime dream of working in a state-of-the-art TV studio like yours."

Self-introduction for a presentation

"Good morning. My name is Pamela Smith and I'm the human interest Editor and chief media consultant for Norrander consults. I've always been zealous about discovering smart ways to do an organized media campaign. I believe establishing an in-house media management strategy within an organization is the first step towards achieving success. I began using in-house strategies myself when I became the media consultant for my company, and now the company has over 10 million clients within the country. That number is increasing

daily, and I'm here to educate you on how to achieve a successful organizational media campaign, too."

> **Self-introduction for a new connection☐**

"My name is Pamela, and I'm the human interest editor and chief media consultant for Norrander consults. We're inventing several innovative media campaigns designed to attract new customers in and outside the country. I've been recruiting young specialist that want to get involved in these projects. I love discussing with people and learning further about

what they usually seek before they patronize a particular product or service."□

Written Self-introduction Sample

Hi, Elizabeth □

My name is Pamela Smith. I'm the human interest editor and chief media consultant for Norrander consults. I've developed several aggressive media campaign designed to increase the clientele base of major organizations. I see myself as a persistent solution-provider, and I'm at all times looking for a fresh challenge. I've recently noticed that your company is struggling to retain its market share due to an unfavorable competition in the industry; and it seems your company is yet to come up with the right solution. I'd love to talk about your needs in this area and see how I can help, with a succeeding strategy that I'm using."

CONTENTS OF A WINNING RESUME

The overwhelming benefits of having a winning resume cannot be overemphasized, because overtime research has shown that about eight percent of those whose resume is well written ended up being invited for the job interview. So now you know why you need to do it well-to earn yourself that great interview that you have been hoping for.

A winning resume is expected to do half of the self-introduction for you. It will not only increase your chances but often, helps prepare the ground for excellent self-introduction. So you should do your best to make sure that you gave out your finest

> **Remember to include in your resume the following –**
>
> **Simplicity**

Keep it simple in terms of section heading, typography, and coloring, bearing in mind the benefit of white space in a document and how overcrowded write up could be difficult to read.

Use a summary statement

Because it explains the value you can add to the organization rather than an objective statement that informs the employer what you need ☐

Highlight your major skills-

as important as your experience is, so your skills, which should correspond with the required skill for the role

Begin with the most recent experience –

the inverted pyramid style where you start from the biggest to the least; because as an unwritten rule, recruiters value the most recent experiences more, than older ones

Separate each heading

In such a way as to make it easy to read, possibly use bullet numbering rather than a paragraph to list things like responsibilities, accomplishments, etc☐

If necessary add volunteer and related experiences –

your volunteer work and related experiences will not only help in protecting your reputation, or presenting you as having a sound personality, it also shows the level of knowledge that you've gained outside your regular job.

> ## Professional self Introduction and Casual introduction

Remember those days in your elementary school, that your teacher will suddenly ask each person to stand up and introduce themself. Do you still remember that dude that stood up when it got to his turn and said-

"hi. my name is Pamela.", scratches his head, probably hoping that someone else will take it from there.

Honestly, what could be more casual than what the fellow did in the name of the introduction? I don't want you to introduce yourself that way. That's why we're at this time trying to learn. Of a truth, a casual introduction like the example above is not only funny, but it will make you appear stupid.

Also remember that the law of the first impression does not allow a second chance, as you would soon find out when you will come out of that interview saying that if only the panel will just give you a second chance.

Now let's see a professional introduction-

"My name is Pamela, and I'm a professional journalist. My work is to offer employment seekers with specialist guidance on career-related issues. I study a lot and seek advice from recruiting experts so you don't have to. I explain how to overcome the employment process, produce a job-winning resume, top job interview, among others."

Things to know in Professional introduction

Anything you're saying should be relevant

You may be a champion in alcohol consumption unless you're applying for a drinking competition, it feels very odd to hear such. It would have been made a good funny remark at the wrong timing and in a wrong context.

> Don't just say your professional title

Work titles don't indicate much. Candidly, explaining what you do on the job, is excellent

> Show how you have professionally contributed in the industry-

Say how being part of that job space has improved the profession and how you would continue to fill the gap in the overall interest of the profession

> Be innovative about it.

Yes, we know that you've spent a lot of time and money reading about the self-introduction, you have attended few seminars, where some practical were done, and also you think you have mastered the art of the artificial smile. Don't be fooled by all that as nothing is as disappointing as trying to be like others. This means that you have to decide the best way you think can do the magic for you and confidently walk through that.

Get yourself ready-

Never go to an interview unprepared, regardless of the suddenness of the interview, or your self-confidence level. Preparation here could mean different things to different persons. For some, it's as simple as reading a page or two about the interviewer. It will not be a bad idea to rehearse what you intend to say to reduce the odds of being taken by surprise.

Mind the audience.-

Assuming the panel of interviews is made up of a mix- audience local and international. It may even be more difficult to please those who may not interpret your contribution in the right context.

> **Be careful about fun ways of introduction-**

This is so because what you think is funny may not echo the same in others.

> **Watch your body language-**

you don't want to be told at this moment of the benefit of body language in any formal communication. Body language at all times works much more than you can imagine. That's, you need to be mindful of it. You'd never know if it's the only thing your interviewer is hoping to use in scoring you. Now as a rule, always maintain decent eye contact; in time for a handshake, keep it natural; always talk with confidence, and do not fiddle, do a casual eye movement or put up a crossed arms. And remember how you end your speech is more important than how you started it.

> **Sample of a Written self – Introduction to new colleagues or Team**

Before you write down your introduction in the form of a letter, you might as well inquire from some of your colleagues about how they did it prior to this time. And when you start writing, see it as if you're talking to someone. So allow it to flow naturally.

Example " *Hi,*

My name is Pamela. I've just joined the editorial department as a human interest editor.

I'll be studying our house style so that I will contribute my best to this organization.

In case you see a fresh face around, of course, that's me. I'm open to any useful career discussion at my leisure our.

Cheers!

Pamela"

TELL ME MORE ABOUT YOURSELF

This so-called dreaded question can come in different forms, which might include but not limited to the following.

1." walk me through your resume"

1. *"Tell me something about you that is not in your CV"*

2. *"How would you describe yourself"*

Even some experts in interpersonal communication are also nervous at a point when confronted with this question. So it's not entirely out of place to shiver over it simply because you don't know what the interviewer wants to know about you. The important thing here is to know how to provide the answer, and in doing so you must know what to include and what not to include in your answer.□

Join me down the train as I will show you how you can approach this question with relevant samples here-

Preparing your response

In getting ready for an interview it might be very useful to do a little soul searching practices that may include-
☐

What qualities give me more advantage in this role?-

For instance, it might be your experience, specialized training (certifications) or just your technical skills. A careful study of the job description will help you with this. ☐

Why am I interested in this position? –

Think of how the job will possibly fit into your career dream and why you think going for it is the best option.

> ## Know also why you're interested in the organization or the industry

Is it in line with your professional goal and career objective; do you think that you can create an impact in that industry? Or still that you're just excited about the current trend in the industry and want be associated with it. Putting these questions in perspective will help you come up with a formidable response that is in line with your feeling about the job and the company.

> **What quality or characteristic do I have that is best suited for a position like this? –**

Are my a curious personality, overzealous, generous, entrepreneurial, organized, etc. think of how some of the personal qualities add together to give you a unique personality.

Answering The Tell Me About Yourself Question

The way you answer the tell me - about yourself question will determine how the interview will go. Everyone will like to tell a good story about themselves but to say it in two minutes or so in a concise statement is where the problem is. These are a few things you need to consider before providing an answer-

> **Consider including your experiences and successes relating to the position-**

Having read the job description and understood the skills required, make sure that you present a skill that is in line with the requirement- and remembers to start with the most recent ones.'□

> **Determine if there's a link between your current job and the one you want to change to**

Is it a superior position that requires more responsibility or that you're just transiting to a job with a different set of skills. Perhaps a good correlated explanation might pull you through the hurdle.

> **Emphasize on your abilities and strength with specific references**

Always unambiguously present a realistic fact. For instance "I *increased the company's clientele by 50% with an aggressive advert campaign strategy".*

Project your personality

Remember that the main reason for this question is for you to expose your personality, so in trying to market your person ensure that you showcase your intellectual prowess and personal development, which you can do in a way that makes you sociable through a professionally acceptable tone of communication.

☐

> ## Sample Of Tell Me About Yourself Response

Though everyone's response in a given situation will not be the same, because we all have our different stories of life circumstances, it may however not be out of place to see how other people responded to the question that you're about to answer.□

You can read through and master how I responded in one of the numerous interviews that I have attended: □

"I started my career in an oil servicing firm as client

relation personnel, but eight years ago I was attracted to the media space. I've always been interestingly attracted to written communication and working as a team. My successful client relations experience made me take up media consultancy; I've been developing a career as a driven media expert for the last seven years.

"In my current role at Norrander consults, the efficiency of the office has been a unique dream especially as

it relates clientele base. Recently I introduced an in-house media campaign team to implement strategic media campaign communication. The immediate result was a 50% increase in company clientele. I'm really satisfied with the outcome of my work.

Anytime that I'm not working, I spend most of my time researching new ideas and trends" ☐

In summary, the Tell-me-about-yourself-question is all about telling your interviewer what he needs to know about you. It's a very good opportunity to put up a sound first impression

> **What to and what not to say in responding to "tell me about yourself" interview situation.**

Conclusively, I have outlined some things you should always remember to include in your answer and the once that are irrelevant.

Always Remember to

- Link personal strength with examples

- Emphasize on details and results that you can measure

- Do not include everything written on your resume

- Remember past experiences and achievements

- Connect your present job description to the position you're applying for

- Avoid very personal details like religions and political views etc.

- Don't say more about the role and the company

- Link your skill with the job description

- If need includes briefly your hobbies, intellectual activities, and community participation □

- Pen down for rehearsal, samples from books and practice it

Remember not to-□

- Give out very personal issues- your life circumstances should not be the reason for hiring you in a job.

- Don't give out more detail than necessary about your strength

- Never try to say word to word, the content of your resume, rather discuss key points ☐

- Don't be hasty to say your intention about the job or how you can gain from it- reserve it for the advance stage of the interview when you're almost certain that you will get the job

HOW TO INTRODUCE YOURSELF IN A GROUP

As we all know, the idea of getting people to know about us can be quite intimidating especially if you're the type that value your personality. The fear of how others will react about what we want to say is an anxious and a nerve-racking task, more so when you're lagging in the current trend in what some will call industrial standard about self-introduction □

I still recall how I use to organize classes for teenagers who came to me with problems of self-introduction and still remembered how they often appear during the practical session; even persons who you think will do very well in it more often than not end as a failure like others. Simply because they're unprofessional or should I say uncomfortable in their introduction.

Then I was quick to forgive their ignorance because I was once like them; with little or knowledge of what to say or how to begin, and more so with no one available to teach me. Hence, I find myself struggling with that obvious anxiety that is characteristic of inexperienced public speakers.

Though now a master in the art, I will not forget in a hurry a scenario some years back that made me take up the challenge of learning and growing from the art of self-introduction. I called it art because, though a simple mannered presentation, it requires a lot of creativity.

It's a day I never wanted to repeat in my history as a communicator. What was the issue? You're already wondering. It's a day I went to defend my final undergraduate thesis in front of a panel that comprises of my

English lecturer who earlier learned that I was among the lucky three that scored an A in his subject.☐

While I will not bother you with a supposed dramatic situation that occurred in the process of my Self-introduction that I later learned was a big flop, I vividly remember that heart-pounding, mind wondering and worrying about how to begin.☐

For this write-up, whether you're expected to do an introduction in a classroom as a **teacher** or a **student,** expected to talk to your **Boss** and **colleagues** in that your **new job**, or simply addressing a

large crowd in a **convention**; apart from the fact that you need to know what constitutes a good introduction and how to go about it- communication experts have identified few methods that you can adopt to help you deliver excellently.

Some of this method is what I will share with you here-

The story sharing method –

you can think of a good story whether real or imagined that did portray you as fun to be with.

Let us use a **teacher's introduction in a classroom** to demonstrate this

First, you need to be reminded that the reason for the introduction in the first place is to let your audience feel at home and be ready to learn from you. This means that you must try to portray yourself as a likable personality.

Now starting with your professional background, your interests and perhaps values would be perfect here; bearing in mind that your introduction is expected to create the right atmosphere for the class to flow.

In this example, you're a senior lecturer that has just been assigned to teach young adult males that are mainly undergraduate students of different higher institutions on a topic in your area of specialization, at a seminar. You would have set the right tone in your introduction if you begin by adding thus

"After I obtained my first degree in sociology and a master degree in social learning, I enroll myself in several non-governmental advocacy programs and today I'm happy to

tell you that though my doctorate is in view I have already published my findings on the research on...(you mention the topic of the seminar) that's why I was selected to speak to you in this seminar"

In the above introductory speech, the lecturer has given a professional background, experiences, and founded interest in issues concerning his audience. He can go further in telling them what he will be doing now if he was in there shoe and why he would do so.☐

I'm telling you, even if you decide to omit certain things because of time, you will soon discover that one or two-person may want you to tell more of certain information about yourself. That is how to know when you've made an impact in your introduction.

Providing memorable information-

I agreed that the aim of self-introduction is just to establish credibility, you must also look towards establishing bond by providing relatable information. Do you still remember how you identify people based on what you heard about them? That's how your intro should make your audience feel about you. They should always remember you base on what you said. That's why some persons are given a nomenclature after listening to them. For instance, you must have heard some students call their teacher "a no-nonsense fellow". That's how they summarize his or her personality.□

This method is even more powerful if you have something in common with your audience. In the foregoing scenario that I painted above about the teacher, the lecturer may say

"I'm Pamela Smith, I'm a communication expert, but any time

I'm on holiday I also spend most of my time attending seminars."

Remember that you must not share something too personal or talk about something that may divide your audience —like politics, religion, etc. rather you should stick to things that draw everyone together.☐

Have fun-

Another subtle method to make your information penetrate easily and make your audience feel at home with you is to make fun. Now you can start by saying

"I'd like to introduce you to Mr. Pamela Smith, ladies call him Franky because he cannot hurt a fly; though some still reject his advances."

Self Introduction in a Conference

Base on the discussion so far, you can at least say that you now know what it means to self-introduce yourself. Why the term is the same at all times, different formal settings and circumstances require different approaches.

In other words, you have to know the most appropriate way to identify yourself at any giving time, especially in a public event like conferences, symposiums, and any of such formal group discussion. The focus here is, when you're attending as a participant in any corporate meeting, your introduction should focus on your role in the conference and what you tend to gain from the event.

Let's say you're a media consultant at a client relations conference. You can start by saying

"Hi, I'm Pamela, Pamela Smith and I'm the client relations officer for Norrander consults. I'd like to know more about how to consistently

satisfy a loyal customer through targeted communication."

SELF INTRODUCTION BOOSTING MOTIVATIONAL QUOTES OF ALL TIME

A Quote is said to be very influential when it creates an impact, it's usually outlive the creator and handed down from generation to generation. If you have not been affected by the power of a quote at one time or the other in your life, I think it is high time you read more books. Because it's either you have not been reading or that you need to read more. Quotes are not just words, they make known powerful ideas that reverberate with our very core.

A very important reason why I love quotes is how relevant it can be. Though often comes in an unsophisticated manner it's usually an embodiment of wisdom.

I also believe that quotes help us to be better persons in a society; and so, whether it's for self-inspiration or the fun of it they following quotes have made a thoughtful positive impact in my life and I'm certain it will do so for you.

Read through these famous quotes, and remember to apply it in your daily life-

"Love For All, Hatred For None." – **Khalifatul Masih III**

"Change the world by being yourself." – **Amy Poehler**

"Every moment is a fresh beginning." – **T.S Eliot**

"I don't need it to be easy, I need it to be worth it." – **Lil Wayne**

"Never let your emotions overpower your intelligence." – **Drake**

"Nothing lasts forever but at least we got these memories." – **J. Cole**

"Don't you know your imperfections is a blessing?" – **Kendrick Lamar**

"Let the beauty of what you love to be what you do." – **Rumi**

"What we think, we become." – **Buddha**

"All limitations are self-imposed." – **Oliver Wendell Holmes**

"Tough times never last but tough people do." – **Robert H. Schiuller**

"Problems are not stopped signs, they are guidelines." – **Robert H. Schiuller**

"One day the people that don't even believe in you will tell everyone how they met you." – **Johnny Depp**

"If I'm gonna tell a real story, I'm gonna start with my name." – **Kendrick Lamar**

"If you tell the truth you don't have to remember anything." – **Mark Twain**

"Have enough courage to start and enough heart to finish."– **Jessica N. S. Yourko**

"Never regret anything that made you smile."– **Mark Twain**

"Die with memories, not dreams." – **Unknown**

"Aspire to inspire before we expire." – **Unknown**

"Everything you can imagine is real." – **Pablo Picasso**

"Simplicity is the ultimate sophistication." – **Leonardo da Vinci**

"Whatever you do, do it well."– **Walt Disney**

"Hate comes from intimidation, love comes from appreciation."- **Tyga**

"I could agree with you but then we'd both be wrong." – **Harvey Specter**

"Oh, the things you can find, if you don't stay behind." – **Dr. Seuss**

"Determine your priorities and focus on them." – **Eileen McDargh**

"Be so good they can't ignore you." – **Steve Martin**

"Dream as if you'll live forever, live as if you'll die today." – **James Dean**

"Yesterday you said tomorrow. Just do it." – **Nike**

"May your choices reflect your hopes, not your fears." – **Nelson Mandela**

"A happy soul is the best shield for a cruel world." – **Atticus**

"White is not always light and black is not always dark." – **Habeeb Akande**

"Reality is wrong, dreams are for real." – **Tupac**

"To live will be an awfully big adventure." – **Peter Pan**

"Try to be a rainbow in someone's cloud." – **Maya Angelou**

"There is no substitute for hard work." – **Thomas Edison**

"What consumes your mind controls your life"- **Unknown**

"Strive for greatness." – **Lebron James**

"Wanting to be someone else is a waste of who you are." – **Kurt Cobain**

"And still, I rise." – **Maya Angelou**

"The time is always right to do what is right." – **Martin Luther King Jr.**

"If the world was blind how many people would you impress?" – **Boonaa Mohammed**

"I will remember and recover, not forgive and forget." – **Unknown**

"The meaning of life is to give life meaning." – **Ken Hudgins**

"Life becomes easier when you learn to accept the apology you never got". – **R. Brault**

"Happiness depends upon ourselves." – **Aristotle**

"Turn your wounds into wisdom." – **Oprah Winfrey**

"Change the game, don't let the game change you." – **Macklemore**

"It hurt because it mattered." – **John Green**